THE SECRETS OF SKIN COLOUR BOOK 1

Rita Bhandari

Illustrated by
Indra Audipriatna

 FriesenPress

One Printers Way
Altona, MB R0G 0B0
Canada

www.friesenpress.com

Copyright © 2022 by Rita Bhandari
First Edition — 2022

Illustrations by Indra Audipriatna

www.acecompeers.com

All rights reserved.

No part of this publication may be reproduced in any form, or by any means, electronic or mechanical, including photocopying, recording, or any information browsing, storage, or retrieval system, without permission in writing from FriesenPress.

ISBN
978-1-03-910871-4 (Hardcover)
978-1-03-910870-7 (Paperback)
978-1-03-910872-1 (eBook)

1. *Juvenile Nonfiction, Diversity & Multicultural*

Distributed to the trade by The Ingram Book Company

MEET THE ACE COMPEERS!

The Ace Compeer Series provides parents and teachers with meaningful stories and educational discussion questions to help children better understand our world and the people in it. As a whole, this series teaches about equity and inclusion and nurtures children's natural hunger for knowledge.

Using kid-friendly language and science, this first book of the series uses inquiry-based learning to encourage critical thinking and antiracist ideas. As you read on, you will meet Erika (she/her), Ang (he/him), Basma (she/her), Riley (they/them), and Manjeet (he/him).

Though the Ace Compeers are all different, they stand united together. There's a reason why they call themselves the Compeers! Do you know what COMPEER means?

> "Compeer is a noun that means
> a person of equal rank or status"
> EQUAL, PEER
> OR
> COMPANION

PART ONE!
OUR INSTRUCTION MANUALS

OPEN YOUR EYES,

READY YOUR EARS,

IT'S TIME TO LEARN,

WITH THE ACE COMPEERS!

Look, Ang has something to say.

"What's our mission today, Ang?" asks Basma.

"Well," says Ang, "Today we are going to learn all there is to know about our physical characteristics!"

"All humans have a lot in common," says Ang. "We all have eyes, hair, hands, and loads of other stuff. These are called similarities."

"We're with you so far," says Basma.

"Great!" Ang continues.

"We also have lots of differences. For example, we all have different heights, hair colours, body types, and skin colours. Differences, you see?"
"Talk about the new stuff, Ang!" says Riley playfully.
"Okay, okay. All of these things you can see, the differences and the similarities, are called physical characteristics," says Ang.

"Wait!" says Basma. "So everybody is different and the same? Is that what you're saying, Ang?"

"Um . . . yes." Ang seems less sure now. "On the inside, we all have blood and bones and organs, but we look different on the outside."

Basma is confused.
Erika thinks blood is gross.
But Riley has something important to say.

"Makes sense to me!" says Riley. "Of course we all look different. It would be very confusing if we all looked the same."

"You guys know about our physical characteristics, right? That we all have some things that are the same and some things that are different?"

6

"See," says Riley. "They already knew that!"

"Great!" says Ang. "Well then, if they already know, then our mission is complete! I'm starving. Who wants to grab lunch? I'm thinking the Caribbean roti place at the end of my street. Let's go!"

"Hold on, Ang," says Erika. "You're not getting away that easy. We're the Ace Compeers! They want answers, and we're here to deliver them. We can do better!" shouts Erika dramatically.

"Don't worry, guys. Erika to the rescue!"

Okay, Compeers, let's start at the very beginning. We get our human characteristics from our genes," explains Erika. "A gene is an inheritance unit of a cell that we get from our biological parents."

"Huh?" says Riley.
"I'm hungry," moans Ang.

"That's a lot of big words, Erika," says Basma. "We don't know what you're talking about."

"Ha, sorry, guys." Erika laughs. "I get carried away sometimes. Let me try and explain again."

"Okay, so, the thing that makes us the way we are, including what makes all our similarities and differences, is found in our DNA," explains Erika. "We all have great big instruction manuals, and everybody's manual is different."

"Our manuals are very long and detailed, and some of the pages are instructions for what we look like. There's a page for everything: one page for eye colour, one for height, one for skin colour, and so on. That's what our genes are."

"Cool!" shouts Riley. "Do you think, if I put my favourite purple jeans on, my eyes will change colour?" Riley whispers to themself. "I knew my jeans were magic," they say.

"Not those kinds of jeans," says Erika. "The genes we are talking about today are part of our bodies and are so tiny we can't see them."

"What has this got to do with our physical characteristics?" asks Basma.

"Our genes carry information about lots of different things, including our physical characteristics; what we look like. If we want to know why people look different or similar, we need to understand more about our genetic 'instruction manuals,'" explains Erika.

"One of the pages in our genetic instruction manual is for skin colour. It's only ONE page in the ginormous manual, but skin covers our whole body, so everybody notices it. So let's focus on that. It's one of the biggest differences people notice about each other."

"But it's not such a big difference," says Erika, "because skin colour is only one page.

Two people with light beige skin can have more differences in their manual than a person with light beige skin and a person with dark brown skin.

"So, two white people can be more genetically different than a white and Black person?" asks Basma.

Erika has a sparkle in her eye. "Whoa, look who's using big words now! Yes, that's right! Two people with peach-coloured skin can have similar instructions on the page about skin tone but have a lot of differences on all of the other pages."

"Ah. So, skin colour doesn't make us that different on the inside?" asks Riley.

"That's right," says Erika.

"Oh, oh!" says Ang excitedly. "I was learning about water—"
"Water?" interrupts Riley. "What's water got to do with it?"

"You know how snow and ice are both water?" asks Ang.

"Yes?" says Basma.

"We aren't talking about water." Riley giggles.

"Well," Ang continues, "one is white and fluffy, and the other is see-through and hard, but they're both water. They look different but are all made of water!"

"So, people with different skin colours are like snow, ice, hail, slush—all different looking but made of the same stuff!

"On the other hand, water and vinegar look the same, but are actually quite different. Trust me . . . I know from personal experience." Ang shudders, remembering a time when he accidentally drank vinegar. "You can't just think they are the same because they look the same to you," he adds.

"Ang, your mind works in mysterious ways." Basma giggles. "But I understand it. Let's check our manuals!"

"Hmmm . . . hair colour, ear size, other traits . . . yes, Ang's manual explains a lot."

"Hey, Basma, we have loads in common!"
"See, like ice and snow!"

"Explained like a true member of the Ace Compeers! Now, let's keep going.

Here's another cool fact about your skin. Did you know that your skin is an adaptation? Do you know what an adaptation is?"

"When we talk about adaptations in science, we are usually talking about other animals and not the human animal," explains Erika.

"That's odd," whispers Riley to themself. "Wouldn't we want to know more stuff like this about humans? I mean, it's all about us, after all." They are very confused.

"Can you think of another animal that has adaptations?" continues Erika.

"Can we hurry up?" complains Ang. "I'm so hungry for roti my stomach is going to eat itself!"

"I've got this one!" says Basma. "I learned about these cool birds called finches from the Galápagos Islands! The shape and size of their beaks changed over hundreds of years, because they adapted to the foods that were available where they lived."

"Some finches had long, pointed beaks for picking seeds out of cactus fruits, and other finches that lived somewhere else had shorter beaks for eating seeds off the ground. The changes in the shape and size of their beaks were adaptations. They adapted their beaks to suit their environment!"

"Lucky finches, getting to eat food," grumbles Ang.

"Wait," Riley says, looking confused. "If our skin is an adaptation, that means it changes based on our environment. But didn't Erika say that skin colour is a part of our genetic manuals?"

"How can our skin colour be an adaptation if it was written in our genetic instruction manuals before we were born?"

"Yeah," Basma says, curious. "We all live in the same place. Why don't we all have the same skin tone?"

"And why do different shades of skin even exist in the first place?" asks Riley.

"Guys, I'm still so hungry. I'm going to pass out!" whines Ang.

"Okay Ang," Erika smirks. "Let's take a brain break and go and get some roti. But when we get back, you guys had better put helmets on, because without them, your minds will be BLOWN!"

"YESSS!" shouts Ang, relieved.

PART ONE: MAIN IDEAS AND DISCUSSION QUESTIONS

For the educator, parent, or guardian:

Main Goal:

For the reader to understand that there is no biological basis for race. Making assumptions based on skin colour does not make sense, because we all have similarities and differences and skin tone is only one of many human traits.

Main Ideas:

- Everyone has differences and similarities.

- The similarities and differences that we can see are called physical characteristics.

- The most noticeable physical characteristic is skin colour because it covers our bodies, but it is only one of many human traits.

- Two people with light beige skin can have more differences in their manual than a person with light beige skin and a person with dark brown skin. Therefore, there is no biological basis for race.

A Deeper Understanding:

Skin colour and race are not the same thing. Race is socially constructed. That means that the many meanings attached to skin colour were invented. We can certainly see skin colour, but just like eye colour or height, skin colour does not determine personality, intelligence, behaviour, worth, or any other trait society has wrongfully attributed to various skin tones.

Suggested questions to discuss with your child(ren) or students:

- Why does Erika say that in order to understand skin colour, we first need to understand our "genetic instruction manuals"? (page 13)

- Why is it important to know that two people with the same skin colour can be far more genetically different from each other than two people with different skin tones? (page 15)

- Ang uses water to explain different skin tones. Can you think of another way to explain it?

- When comparing water and vinegar, Ang says, "You can't just think they are the same because they look the same to you." Can you apply this sentence to skin colour? Why or why not?

- Is it fair to think that people with the same skin tone have the same personalities, behaviours, beliefs, intelligence, or worth? Why not?

- Why is it important to talk about the difference between skin tone and race?

Note to parents, guardians, and educators: Please read the sections above called Main Goal and A Deeper Understanding before moving on to the discussion questions. Please note that these are suggested discussion questions. You should always preview the questions prior to asking them. Please use your parental discretion or professional judgement when choosing questions that meet your child(ren)'s or students' needs or age bracket.

BRAIN BREAK!

THE AUTHOR SUGGESTS TAKING A BREAK PRIOR TO READING PART TWO OF THE STORY.

PART TWO!
THE POWER OF MELANIN

"Wow!" Basma smiles. "I was really enjoying learning about why we all have different skin tones, but I'm so glad we took this brain break!"

"Yeah, you were right, Ang," adds Riley. "This roti is sooo tasty."

"Told you," says Ang.

"Look," says Erika. "It's our fellow Ace Compeer, Manjeet!"

"Greetings, Compeers," Manjeet says. "Mmmmm! That smells delicious! What'd I miss?"

"Hey, Manjeet," says Basma. "We've been having an awesome time with our new mission: learning all about the physical characteristics of humans."

"I started it," says Ang, "but then I got hungry."

"So, I took over," interrupts Erika.

"Just like always, then!" Manjeet laughs.

"It was so interesting," says Riley. "Erika explained that we all have something called DNA, which is like a gigantic genetic instruction manual. It's full of instructions about who we are, including what we look like. There's a page for everything—hair type, height, even skin colour!"

"We've been learning a lot about skin colour," says Ang. "Did you know that skin colour is an adaptation?"

"Huh?" says Manjeet, confused.

"Yes," continues Ang. "Our skin colour changes based on our environment, just like the beaks of these birds from . . . the North Pole, was it?"

"No, silly," laughs Basma. "The Galápagos Islands! That's nowhere near the North Pole—it's on the equator! Maybe we need to do a geography lesson too."

"Funny you say that, Basma," says Erika, "because our mission cannot be completed without looking at a map!"

"Wait." Ang is confused. "What does geography have to do with it?"

"You'd be surprised," says Erika. "Lots of topics and subjects are connected, like a massive web."

"Science, geography, social studies, history, health, environmental studies—they are all connected. Skin colour is about geography too. That's why we need to look at a map!"

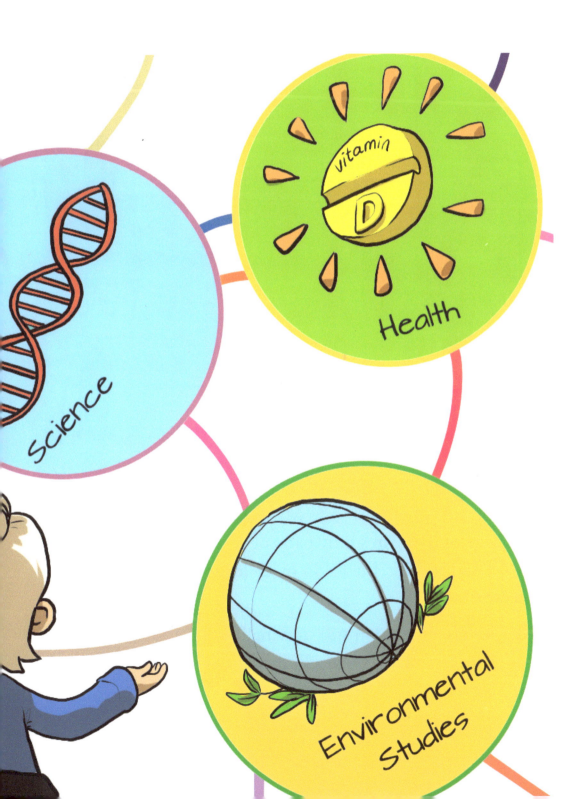

"Oh, I heard about this!" says Manjeet. "A long time ago, humans living in sunny parts of the world adapted to have darker skin. Their skin made loads of something called melanin."

"Melon? Yes, please! I'm still starving." says Ang.
"No, Ang, *melanin*. It's like a built-in sunscreen for your skin," says Manjeet.

"Cool!" say Ang and Riley.

"That's right, Manjeet," adds Erika. "You see, melanin protects us from the sun's rays, and the type and amount of melanin we have is what causes different skin colours."

"Makes sense! If you live somewhere that is very sunny, you'll need more protection from the sun.

So that's why humans who lived closer to the equator, where it's very sunny, adapted to have more melanin, and those who moved farther away adapted to have less."

"But look at us!" says Basma.

"Why do we have different skin tones even though we live in the same environment with the same amount of sunshine?"

"I'm confused again," cries Riley.

"Aha!" says Erika. "Well, that's because it can take thousands of years for adaptation to happen and to be passed onto the next generation of babies." "What?" asks Basma. "Adaptation is passed on in our genes?"

"Oh yes," replies Erika. "An adaptation is only an adaptation if it can be passed onto the next generation through their genes."

"You're doing that thing where you get carried away with your words again Erika! You might have to explain some more," says Manjeet, confused.

"Ha ha! Okay then." Erika laughs. "So, even though our skin colour is already written in our genetic instruction manuals, skin colour is still an adaptation."

"We did adapt to our environments once upon a time. It just took a looong time for the changes to happen!"

"Long ago, our great-great-great-great—and thousands more times great—grandparents passed their genes onto their kids, and those kids passed their genes onto their kids, and that went on and on for thousands of years. Sometimes in our manuals there were words that were added or erased," explains Erika.

"I understand! Over time, certain pages of the manual, like the one about skin colour, changed to adapt to the environment," adds Manjeet. "But, as we have learned, the reason why we now all have different skin tones is that we moved or were moved around the globe way quicker than our skin managed to adapt!"

"So, you know my favourite coding game, *Robot Monster*?'" interrupts Ang.

"Huh? We aren't talking about computer games, Ang," says Riley.

"It's just like coding a computer game!" exclaims Ang. "It's like genes are codes, but for us. It's coding for humans. Awesome!"

"Ang!" Erika is impressed. "You really surprise me with the connections you make sometimes. That was brilliant!"

Ang blushes.

"So, let me get this straight," says Basma. "We adapted different skin tones because it was a way to protect us from the sun?"

"Well, that's part of it, yes," replies Erika. "But there are other reasons too."

Vitamin D

"Like vitamin D!" shouts Manjeet with excitement. "I looked this up yesterday! Our skin helps us to get vitamin D from the sun, right?"

"I heard vitamin D was really important for keeping our bodies healthy and our bones strong," adds Riley.

"Well done! You're both right!" says Erika. "Some scientists believe that our ancestors who lived in places with less sun also needed lighter skin because it is better for absorbing Vitamin D than darker skin."

"The sunlight gives us vitamin D, but it also shines UV rays onto us, which can be harmful to our bodies. Our skin is so clever. It has had to adapt to let just the right amount of sunlight in."

"Wow. I never knew skin was so complicated," says Ang.

"What happens when we get a tan in the summer?" asks Riley.

"Well," answers Erika, "remember melanin? That built-in sunscreen that causes our different skin tones?"
Riley nods.

"When the sun is stronger, our skin needs a bit more protection. So our skin produces more melanin, which, in turn, makes our skin darker," explains Erika. "It's the same stuff that causes different skin colours, but a tan is only temporary."
"And you should still wear sunscreen lotion when the sun is strong," adds Manjeet.

"So," says Basma, "human skin tones have adapted in many different ways for thousands of years. These adaptations could have been affected by the sun's UV rays and by vitamins in our bodies. Is that right?"

"That's right!" says Erika. "And scientists are discovering new things about skin every day."

"Did you know that Africa has the most genetic diversity in the world? There are so many different genetic instruction manuals here!

We have to remember that there are differences in physical characteristics, including skin colour, everywhere in the world," says Manjeet.

"Wow, that's so cool. Skin is amazing," says Ang.

"How can something so awesome cause so many problems in the world?" asks Manjeet, sad.
"What do you mean?" asks Riley.

"Well," answers Manjeet, "many problems are caused when people think they can know stuff about other people just by looking at them. But maybe that is a lesson for another time."

"I think we just found our next mission," says Basma. Riley nods.

"Well done, Compeers!" shouts Riley. "I think this mission is complete. Let's go for dessert! I know where we can get some delicious baklava."

"Great idea!" Ang is excited. "I just need to make a stop to change into my stretchy pants!"

THE COMPEERS CHANT,

"ANOTHER LESSON LEARNED,

WITH US, THE ACE COMPEERS,

REST YOUR BRAINS, CLOSE YOUR BOOKS,

AND GIVE YOURSELF THREE CHEERS!"

PART TWO: MAIN IDEAS AND DISCUSSION QUESTIONS

For the educator, parent, or guardian:

Main Goal:

For the reader to understand that skin tone is a human adaptation. Skin tones changed as a way to keep our species healthy by adapting to have the right amount of vitamin D, while also protecting us from the sun's ultraviolet (UV) rays. The skin's adaptive qualities formed over thousands of years are remarkable and should not have any other meaning attached to it. Unfortunately, as we know, that is not the case in society, and false interpretations of skin tone have had and still have dire consequences.

Main Ideas:

- Skin colour is an adaptation, just like the adaptations of other animals.

- Sun exposure is what influenced this adaptation.

- Humans that lived where it was very sunny benefited from darker skin because the melanin acted as a natural sunscreen, protecting them from harmful UV rays.

- Humans that lived where there was less sun exposure benefited from having lighter skin to help them take in more vitamin D and did not need the added melanin protection from UV rays.

- In today's time, we have sunscreen and vitamin D supplements, so we are lucky enough not to worry about adaptations making some of us better or worse suited to our environments.

- Our genes—our "genetic instruction manuals"—can change over time, and that's exactly what happened with skin colour.

- These changes can take thousands of years to develop.

- Genetic research on skin tone is a lot more complicated and scientists are still discovering new findings.

- The most important thing to remember about skin colour is that it is all about the amount of melanin we have. It has nothing to do with behaviour, personality, worth, capability, or intelligence.

A Deeper Understanding:

After reading both Parts One and Two of the story, we now know that the concept of race is scientifically nonexistent and made up by people (i.e., race is a social construct). Although that is true, the false meanings placed upon skin tone have severe implications. They have affected Black and Indigenous people and people of colour for generations and continue to do so. We can't ignore the lived experiences of all people of colour just because race is a social construct. Race (i.e., grouping people into categories based on physical characteristics like skin tone) has no scientific grounding, but it has real tangible effects on people's lives every day. Race is not biologically real, but it is socially real. The idea that race *shouldn't* matter does not mean that race does not matter. More on this in the next Ace Compeers book!

Suggested discussion questions with your child(ren) or students:

- Why does Erika say that they need to look at a map to help understand skin colour? (page 5)

- Erika explains that many topics and subjects are connected. Looking at the illustration on pages 6 and 7, how can you explain this in your own words? Can you think of other topics or subjects that are connected to one another? How are they connected?

- What is melanin? (pages 8 and 9)

- Why did humans in sunny parts of the world have more melanin? (page 10)

- What happens when you get a tan? (page 21)

- Take a look at the illustration found on pages 24 and 25 and answer the following questions:

    a) What do you think Manjeet means when he says, "Many problems are caused when people think they can know stuff about other people just by looking at them"? Pick one or two people holding up the signs and explain in your own words.

    b) The Ace Compeers are all holding hands at the bottom of the page. Notice the expression on their faces. What does this mean to you?

Note to parents, guardians, and educators: Please read the sections above called Main Goal and A Deeper Understanding before moving on to the discussion questions. Please note that these are suggested discussion questions. You should always preview the questions prior to asking them. Please use your parental discretion or professional judgement when choosing questions that meet your child(ren)'s or students' needs or age bracket.

SOURCES

Basic Concepts in Genetics. (2021). Galapagos Conservation Trust. http://evolution.discoveringgalapagos.org.uk/evolution-zone/galapagos-adaptations/introduction-to-genetics-and-adaptation/genetics-adaptation-darwin/#:%7E:text=Through%20reproduction%2C%20genes%20are%20passed,suited%20to%20the%20new%20environment.&text=Over%20the%20course%20of%20several,the%20needs%20of%20the%20environment

Chou, V. C. (2017, April 17). *How Science and Genetics are Reshaping the Race Debate of the 21st Century.* Harvard Universty. https://sitn.hms.harvard.edu/flash/2017/science-genetics-reshaping-race-debate-21st-century/

Cromie, W. J. (2006, July 24). How Darwin's finches got their beaks. *Harvard Gazette.* https://news.harvard.edu/gazette/story/2006/07/how-darwins-finches-got-their-beaks/#:%7E:text=Darwin%20wondered%20about%20the%20changes,to%20survive%20on%20available%20food

Deng, L., & Xu, S. (2017). Adaptation of human skin color in various populations. *Hereditas, 155*(1), 1–6. https://doi.org/10.1186/s41065-017-0036-2

Equal Earth Wall Map. (2018). Equal Earth. http://equal-earth.com/index.html

LaBracio, L. L. (2016, March 22). *The Science of Skin Color.* TEDEd. https://blog.ed.ted.com/2016/03/22/the-science-of-skin-color-in-ted-ed-gifs/

National Geographic Society. (2019, June 5). *Adaptation.* https://www.nationalgeographic.org/encyclopedia/adaptation/

NIH. (2019, March 13). *Human Genome Project FAQ.* National Human Genome Research Institute. https://www.genome.gov/human-genome-project/Completion-FAQ#:%7E:text=Each%20chromosome%20contains%20hundreds%20to,an%20average%20of%20three%20proteins

ABOUT THE AUTHOR

From a young age, Rita Bhandari's French Canadian and South Asian background fostered in her a deep curiosity about race. Her biracial identity and lived experiences have fueled her curiosity about the science and history of race and inspired her to become an educator and advocate for equity and inclusion. Rita has been teaching for ten years and earned three certificates from the Equity Literacy Institute and a professional Diversity and Inclusion certificate from Cornell University. Rita lives in Toronto, Canada, with her husband and three-year-old toddler.

www.acecompeers.com

CPSIA information can be obtained
at www.ICGtesting.com
Printed in the USA
LVHW070417170322
713683LV00009B/307